Letters

to my

GrandDaughter

____

with Love,

____

Made in United States
North Haven, CT
16 October 2023

42825791R00078